The Greatness Effect

Creating the Life Shift
That Will
Lead to Your Greatest Self

By

Timothy Wallace

The Greatness Effect

*To my family and friends for their love and
support throughout my journey.*

*To you for your support in the accomplishment of my dream of helping
people all over the world find happiness and personal freedom.*

Acknowledgments

I would first like to thank Benjamin Swihart for his incredible support in transforming my manuscript into what it is today. His insight and eye for content were invaluable. I would also like to thank both Patrick Harbula and Donna Johnson-Klonsky for their guidance throughout the process of my writing this book as well as during my self-improvement journey. Your friendship and mentoring are greatly appreciated.

Finally I would like to thank Jessica Medina, Nicholas Sanchez, Chagala Smith, and Justin Wingate for their review of various parts of the manuscript and the great and helpful feedback they gave me, as well as everyone else who supported me throughout the entire process. The realization of this dream of mine would not have been realized without your assistance.

Thank you so much!

Introduction

Life is beautiful, scary, amazing, chaotic, and the single great-est blessing we have been given. There are times throughout our lives when we allow false realities to make us forget just how much of a blessing it truly is. We go from the days of our youth, believing we can achieve anything, focused pri-marily on what makes us happy, to living our lives trapped behind walls of fear and doubt. Living this way will never al-low us to realize the unlimited potential locked within us, and the amazing and fulfilling lives we could have—lives we thought achievable only by the rich, powerful, or lucky. You may be asking yourself in this moment, How do I tap back into that wellspring of hope and positivity?

The answer is simple. You create a Shift. A Shift is a change in mindset and viewpoint that restores your own faith in yourself and humanity, develops a willingness and desire to love yourself, empowers you to strive to become your greatest self, and brings about myriad other great changes. To put it directly, the Shift is a series of small steps and decisions, which I refer to in the book as "Micro Shifts," that ultimately create a change in your psychology and give you a greater sense of optimism and control over the various areas of your life. You achieve this Shift by fo-cusing your thoughts not on the false realities that cause you to recede from your dreams and vision, but rather up-on those outcomes you feel are going to allow you to achieve progress and move in the direction you want to go in your life. Once you've done this, you follow up those thoughts with the corresponding actions that are going to bring about those positive changes.

Speaking of shifts, when you look at a diamond and a lump of coal it would never cross your mind that they are both composed of the same main element. There are three key factors that distinguish a diamond from coal: high levels of heat, extreme pressure, and the non-existence of impurities. These differences are not unlike the differences between one who has yet to find the path and one who is on the journey to achieving self–mastery: the ability to control one's emotions (heat), being able to face defeat, fear, and failure and keep going (pressure), and a determination to eliminate or come to terms with the negative areas of one's life and live with integrity (non-existence of impurities). There is a point in your life when you must make the decision to stop holding yourself back and create the shift that will allow you to find the diamond within yourself.

My self-improvement journey began like several others, with a burning desire to change my life and discover and fulfill my purpose. Before beginning my "true" journey I had to overcome a life that was filled with adversity. A few of those obstacles included the loss of several family members including my mother, father, and younger sister, as well as being physically and psychologically abused in my youth. As difficult as those experiences were to triumph over, I would say the most difficult obstacle I've had to overcome was coming to the belief that someone such as myself, coming from my humble upbringing, being told that I had a mental deficiency, and years of self-loathing, could ever step out of the shadow of mediocrity or know and achieve true love, happiness, and greatness.

Several years ago I made the decision to join the United States Navy, a decision that would give me the sense of direction I needed and change my life forever. One of the first and greatest lessons I learned when I joined the service is that the mind can either be your greatest ally or your worst enemy. When I found myself facing a challenge or obstacle, no matter what it was, an internal battle would commence. With the guidance and support of my mentors I learned how to focus and gain control of the direction I would allow my mind to go during these battles. Coupling this skill with the principles and philosophies I've learned throughout my journey has helped me create a dynamic Shift in my life that I felt compelled to share with others. This compulsion led me to the discovery of my *life's purpose* (one of the essential ingredients to achieving greatness) and the start of my "true" journey. As a Self-Mastery Coach I have dedicated myself to teaching others how they too can take control of their destinies and bring more love, peace, and happiness into their lives. This book is meant to do just that.

In the following pages, you will find a series of concepts, ideas, principles, and generally positive and motivational information which—if fully utilized and approached as advised—will inspire you to create positive and constructive change.

In order to get the most from *The Greatness Effect*, the following method should be followed:

- Before reading each day's message, put yourself into a mindset of open-mindedness.

- Eliminate all thoughts of fear, doubt, judgement and expectation.

- Understand that you are capable of anything, are worthy of self-love, and that the only reality that exists in this world, whether good or bad, is the one you choose to believe.

- (If able) Go to a place that is quiet and that you find peaceful.

- Read the day's Micro Shift both at the start and the end of the day.

- Focus on the Power Phrase throughout the day.

- Complete/execute the Activities for Insight.

- Create one or more action steps that are in alignment with the day's Micro Shift.

- Have fun and trust the process.

Like any other endeavor in life, you will get what you put into it, and if you commit to making this book a part of your daily routine you *will* experience positive changes in your life. I commend you for making the *decision* to take this journey to change your life for the better. May the fulfillment of your highest goals, dreams, and desires be achieved. I look forward to working with you throughout your journey.

∞

The journey of a thousand miles
begins with a single step.

—*Lao Tzu*

Micro Shift #1

How badly do you want to achieve Greatness? Would you say that it is worth a little blood, sweat, tears, sleepless nights, or facing certain fears?

Greatness might mean different things to you—financial freedom, happiness and security for you and your family, or finding the person you want to spend the rest of your life with. However you define Greatness for your life, you must fight for the things that you truly want, and always keep in mind WHY they are so important to you.

Today's Power Phrase:

I will not give up on my goals and dreams.

Insight Activity:

How do you define Greatness in your own life? What do you want? What are you willing to bear in your fight for it?

_____

_____

_____

_____

_____

_____

_____

_____

_____

_____

_____

_____

_____

_____

_____

Micro Shift #2

Are you aware that you are in complete control of your emotions? Your being happy, frustrated, angry, or sad are all decisions that you must make. Next time you find yourself in a situation causing you to feel unwanted emotions, take a step back from the situation, get a couple of deep breaths in, and recognize that, regardless of the situation, ultimately you want to be happy. You must take control of your happiness.

Today's Power Phrase:

I will take control of my happiness and other emotions.

Insight Activity:

What situations are causing you to be less than happy, or feel you are not in control of your emotions? Today, if you start to feel less than your best, take a moment to notice the thoughts in your head. Ask yourself, What is the next small thing I can do to change this situation?

_____

_____

_____

_____

_____

_____

_____

_____

_____

_____

_____

_____

_____

_____

Micro Shift #3

Have you ever been the recipient of someone else's kindness? Or used your knowledge or skills to help someone? That is one of the beauties of this world. The more you help people and the greater your level of service, the more success you will experience. What needs do you see in this world that have yet to be fulfilled? And of those, which of them are also in alignment with your passion? If you find that particular need, that could be a perfect recipe for success. Remember, you get what you give in this world, so give big in a positive way!

Today's Power Phrase:

I will give the world what I want in return.

Insight Activity:

What two or three needs have you noticed lacking in the world? Have you said to yourself, "Somebody really should do something about . . .?" What's one thing you could do to meet that need that would also fill you with a sense of real achievement?

_____

_____

_____

_____

_____

_____

_____

_____

_____

_____

_____

_____

_____

Micro Shift #4

Do you know what F.E.A.R. stands for? False Evidence Appearing Real. So what are you afraid of? That you're not good enough? That you're not worthy? That you're not ready for the success you know you deserve? How much longer are you going to allow false excuses to prevent you from living the great life that you know deep down you're capable of? Take control of your destiny by not only recognizing your true potential, but also making the necessary changes to your life that will help you make your dreams a reality.

Today's Power Phrase:

I will not allow fear to limit my life.

Insight Activity:

What are you afraid of? What do you "know" you can't do, and why do you tell yourself you can't do this? Now, ask yourself, Are you absolutely positive there is no way on Earth you could ever do the thing you really want? Write at least one reason why that belief might not be accurate.

_____

_____

_____

_____

_____

_____

_____

_____

_____

_____

_____

_____

_____

Micro Shift #5

Your inner voice can be either your greatest Ally or your worst Enemy. It's of paramount importance to remain conscious of the kind of thoughts you allow to dwell in your mind and to also actively shift those thoughts from negative to positive when necessary. This kind of change will not happen overnight but, with consistent practice, you will slowly start to see pessimistic thoughts lose their power over your life.

Today's Power Phrase:

I shall become the master of my thoughts.

Insight Activity:

What do your negative inner thoughts tell you? Have you ever tried writing them down? Try writing three to five of these word for word, as they are in your head. Now, try writing three more accurate, empowered thoughts that can replace these. For practice, try repeating these new thoughts to yourself.

_____

_____

_____

_____

_____

_____

_____

_____

_____

_____

_____

_____

_____

_____

Micro Shift #6

If you have big goals and dreams, or are presented with a great opportunity, don't put it off until tomorrow or be afraid to take a chance. Instead, take full advantage of every opportunity for growth that presents itself. Our time here is much too short for regrets. Understand that you are never too young or too old to have great and exciting experiences or to make great new memories. Get out there and make the most of your life!

Today's Power Phrase:

I will live my life to the fullest.

Insight Activity:

What's one opportunity you missed in the last month or two that keeps coming up in your thoughts in passing moments? What can you do to ensure you say yes to the next great opportunity that comes your way?

_____

_____

_____

_____

_____

_____

_____

_____

_____

_____

_____

_____

_____

_____

Micro Shift #7

If no one has told you so far today, I would like to tell you that you are Awesome! Acts of kindness don't need to be huge. They can be as simple as giving someone a compliment or asking someone how their day is going, or you can be like me and patrol supermarkets for people that need help grabbing things from the top shelf. You never know how a simple act of kindness can completely turn someone's life around. Doing so will not only brighten someone else's day, but yours as well.

Today's Power Phrase:

I will treat others with kindness at every opportunity.

Insight Activity:

As you go throughout your day today, ask yourself, whenever the opportunity presents itself, what act of kindness might I be able to perform?

_____

_____

_____

_____

_____

_____

_____

_____

_____

_____

_____

_____

_____

_____

Happiness can exist only in acceptance.

—*George Orwell*

Micro Shift #8

How much time do you set aside for yourself to have fun? Sometimes we allow ourselves to get so caught up with our work and other areas of our lives that we forget to just sit back and enjoy life. There is absolutely nothing wrong with taking care of business, but as the saying goes, "All work and no play, makes Jack a dull boy." Ensure that you have allotted yourself a sufficient amount of time to enjoy and appreciate life and remember to have fun.

Today's Power Phrase:

It's OK to have fun and enjoy life.

Insight Activity:

What's something fun you've been meaning to do but haven't due to a lack of time? Take out your day planner now and make an appointment to do this and have fun, whether it's five minutes, or a half day.

_____

_____

_____

_____

_____

_____

_____

_____

_____

_____

_____

_____

_____

_____

Micro Shift #9

They say that the definition of Insanity is doing the same thing every day hoping for a change. I'm here to tell you that things will not change until you make the decision to stop standing still, and make the necessary alterations to your life that will allow you to live the way you truly want and deserve to live. If you have set big goals for yourself (and you should!), you can expect the road to be tough. And this is true for anything truly worth having in life. But after you accomplish that goal you will not only realize the depths of your own capabilities, you will also know the gratification that comes from walking the road of progression.

Today's Power Phrase:

I will keep moving forward towards my goals.

Insight Activity:

What is one Big Goal you have for your life right now? Is there some part where you are stuck? What can you do to make a change? Do you need to read something? Take action? Perhaps an e-mail or phone call?

_____

_____

_____

_____

_____

_____

_____

_____

_____

_____

_____

_____

_____

Micro Shift #10

The most foolish person in the world is the one who thinks they know everything. When you are presented with new positive, constructive information, it might be new or it might be something you've heard before. Either way, go into it with an open mind ready to learn. You'll either learn some great new information or you'll validate and reinforce the old. Take full advantage of every opportunity to grow.

Today's Power Phrase:

I will take advantage of every opportunity for growth.

Insight Activity:

When was the last time you heard someone giving you advice and thought to yourself, "I know, I've heard this before?" The next time you find yourself saying this, ask yourself, What's new about their take on this type of situation? Is there some part I might still be missing?

_____

_____

_____

_____

_____

_____

_____

_____

_____

_____

_____

_____

_____

_____

_____

Micro Shift #11

If you are finding yourself complaining about a situation, realize that you are making yourself a victim. Understand that
this is your life and if something is wrong, it is you who
must make the decision to either hold onto those negative
feelings or take new action in the direction of your happiness.

Placing blame for your circumstances on some other
person or circumstance leaves you powerless to make such
change. You must own it, and shift your life accordingly.
Take control of your circumstances.

Today's Power Phrase:

I will own and take control of my circumstances.

Insight Activity:

Pay attention to your conversations, and notice the next time you find yourself complaining about a situation, whether your own challenge, or the world situation at large. Challenge yourself to offer a potential solution, even perhaps saying, "I guess I could possibly . . ." and see if you can name a potential solution.

_____

_____

_____

_____

_____

_____

_____

_____

_____

_____

_____

_____

_____

_____

Micro Shift #12

Nobody in this world is perfect. No matter how great things may be going in your life, keep in mind that you too have faults, have dealt with issues, and have made mistakes.

What would you say there is to gain from thinking of, or even worse speaking to or treating, others in a negative way? We are far more likely to be successful in this world by building one another up as opposed to tearing one another down. Your thoughts and actions should be focused on improving your own situation and, once that is in order, helping others do the same.

Today's Power Phrase:

I will develop a mentality of non-judgement.

Insight Activity:

When was the last time you were tempted to speak negatively of someone or a situation, or perhaps made such a comment? What might instead have been a more constructive response? As you go about your day today, how might you catch yourself before you voice a less-than-positive thought, and give yourself the space to respond differently?

_____

_____

_____

_____

_____

_____

_____

_____

_____

_____

_____

_____

_____

Micro Shift #13

Are you having or have you had a rough day? Have hard times made you feel like just giving up? Circumstances in our lives could always be better, but remember that they could also be worse. What are a few things in your life that you have to be grateful for? The ability to see and read this message? To touch and hold your loved ones? Or more importantly, the ability to wake up and live another day.

With each blessed day, you can move one step closer to the life you desire. With that in mind, stay focused and count your blessings.

Today's Power Phrase:

I will be grateful for each blessing in my life.

Insight Activity:

What are three things you are grateful for in your life right now? In your relationships? Your health? Your occupation or business? Take a few minutes to write these down.

_____

_____

_____

_____

_____

_____

_____

_____

_____

_____

_____

_____

_____

_____

Micro Shift #14

Have you ever thought to yourself, when looking back on past experiences, "If I knew back then what I know now, I would have accomplished so much more?" Picture yourself 20 or 30 years from now; would you be saying something like, "Man, I wish I would have watched some more TV?" Of course not!

Make sure that your future self has absolutely no regrets. The only fear that you should ever have in your life, is that you didn't try to make the most of it.

Today's Power Phrase:

I will live my life to the fullest, with no regrets.

∞

Insight Activity:

What's something on your bucket list you've been wanting to get started on, or been afraid you might regret if you didn't try? What are you going to do to get started? Even if it's a ten-minute step?

_____

_____

_____

_____

_____

_____

_____

_____

_____

_____

_____

_____

_____

_____

We are shaped by our thoughts; we become what we think.
When the mind is pure, joy follows like a shadow that never
leaves.

—*Buddha, in* The
Dhammapada

Micro Shift #15

How many times in your life have you talked your way out of starting or finishing a goal? Do you tell yourself that you don't have the resources, connections, or credentials to achieve something? If so, please stop. Instead, start looking at what you do have, what you are capable of, and what you can and will work towards. Every excuse can be flipped on its head by using new words that encourage you to progress further with your goals.

Today's Power Phrase:

I will take steps (no matter how small), towards my goals every day.

∞

Insight Activity:

Think back to the last time you said to yourself, "I can't do . . ." (the goal or project). What were you "sure" you didn't have that would be needed in order to do it? What can you tell yourself in place of this reason? What's the next doable step toward this goal?

_____

_____

_____

_____

_____

_____

_____

_____

_____

_____

_____

_____

_____

_____

Micro Shift #16

Wherever your journey in life is taking you, never underestimate your own worth. It is important to recognize the areas in your life that are in need of improvement, but it is equally important to recognize how far you have come.

Focusing too much on either will either demoralize you or take away some of that fire that pushes you to progress. Use whatever fuel you can to help you down the road to a greater you.

Today's Power Phrase:

I will always remember how far I have come.

∞

Insight Activity:

List three areas in your life you need to improve . . .

_____

_____

_____

_____

_____

_____

_____

_____

OK, now make a list of your five most recent accomplishments.

_____

_____

_____

_____

_____

_____

_____

_____

Micro Shift #17

Love and happiness are two of life's most precious gifts. They feel great when received and even better when given. The world at times can make you doubt humanity, but please know that there are amazing acts of kindness being done every single day. The golden rule in life is to do to others as you would have them do to you. If you are seeking happiness, if you are seeking peace, if you are hoping to be successful, then help others to achieve those things. Do your part to keep an abundance of positivity in the world.

Today's Power Phrase:

I will give that which I want in my life back to the world.

Insight Activity:

What do you want out of life in this world?

_____

_____

_____

_____

_____

_____

_____

_____

What can you do to help someone else find the same?

_____

_____

_____

_____

_____

_____

_____

_____

_____

Micro Shift #18

Most of the time when you think about investing, you think about finances, but an even greater investment is one that you make in yourself. Whether it's reading a book, sitting in a classroom, or browsing online, you should be constantly in pursuit of knowledge.

With the consistent increase in competitiveness in the job market and the ease of access online for information on any subject you can think of, there is absolutely no reason why you can't become a subject matter expert in your desired field.

KNOWLEDGE IS POWER!

Today's Power Phrase:

I will be sure to invest in knowledge that will assist me in my growth.

∞

Insight Activity:

Take a moment now to look back on what you've written in the way of goals, something you wish you had done differently, or what you'd like to accomplish. Today, either write down the name of someone who's done what you want to do, and ask them to tell you more about their experience or, go on Google and look for one article or video about how to do the thing you need to learn.

_____

_____

_____

_____

_____

_____

_____

_____

_____

_____

_____

_____

_____

Micro Shift #19

Integrity is defined as the quality of being honest and having strong moral principles. So the question I have for you is, What are the principles you live by, and are you living by them? Every day of our lives, we are fighting a battle with ourselves. A battle to establish discipline and control over our lives. The only way to maintain the upper hand in that battle is to understand what integrity means to you and ensure that you are living life in alignment with that.

Today's Power Phrase:

I will live my life in alignment with my morals and principles.

Insight Activity:

What are the three main morals or principles you live by? How will you hold yourself accountable if or when you stray from them?

_____

_____

_____

_____

_____

_____

_____

_____

_____

_____

_____

_____

_____

_____

_____

Micro Shift #20

Have you set healthy boundaries for yourself? Sometimes we unconsciously allow toxic people or situations to negatively affect our lives. People (in most cases) will only push you as far as you are willing to let them.

By establishing an unwavering set of boundaries, you can ensure that the people inside your circle respect you and support your happiness and journey. This will also strengthen your ability to say No to situations which would previously have caused you to step outside those boundaries. Once you have these boundaries established, don't allow anyone or anything to make you waver, especially yourself.

Today's Power Phrase:

I will set healthy, unwavering boundaries.

∞

Insight Activity:

Who is one person with whom you sense you have a less-than-optimum set of boundaries? What boundary might be being crossed, and how? What can you say No to in the situation that will create a healthier boundary with this person, or situation?

_____

_____

_____

_____

_____

_____

_____

_____

_____

_____

_____

_____

_____

Micro Shift #21

Do you ever find yourself doubting your ability to achieve your goals? I have a question for you, What is the smallest, most immediate action you can take to get started towards achieving your primary goal? Speaking from personal experience with battling doubt, when you go from thoughts and words into action, it is like taking a huge gorilla off your back. It's absolutely OK to have big dreams and aspirations, but eventually, you just have to grab the bull by the horns and take action. Any step, no matter how small, in the right direction is what we should all strive for.

Today's Power Phrase:

I will take steps, no matter how small, towards achieving my goals.

∞

Insight Activity:

What are your top three goals at this moment? What are three small actions you can take toward them? Of these three, which is the most doable in the next two days? Which of these will you do next?

_____

_____

_____

_____

_____

_____

_____

_____

_____

_____

_____

_____

_____

_____

Everything you've ever wanted is on the other side of fear.

— *George Adair*

Micro Shift #22

There are several things in this world that can be changed
for the better, but before you decide to help make those
changes you must first look deep within yourself and
address the different areas in your life that need to be
improved. You should also ensure that you are living a life
that is in alignment with your morals and principles. Once
you have done this and achieved balance within your own
life, then you can join, lead, and inspire the various changes
you wish to see in the world.

Today's Power Phrase:

I will improve my own life before taking on the world.

Insight Activity:

What are three changes you want to see in the world? What three changes might you need to make in yourself first to become a better leader? What can you do this week toward these changes?

_____

_____

_____

_____

_____

_____

_____

_____

_____

_____

_____

_____

_____

_____

Micro Shift #23

At times throughout our lives, we have those moments when smiling is the last thing that we want to do, but you might want to re-think that. The act of smiling—in addition to being contagious—activates neural messaging that benefits both your happiness and health.

This happens due to the body's release of dopamine, endorphins, and serotonin (Source: *Psychology Today*). At the end of the day, love and happiness should be the endgame that we pursue. So, remember that you are blessed, smile more, and do what you can to bring more of both in your life.

Today's Power Phrase:

I will do everything I can to smile every day.

∞

Insight Activity:

Today, just remember to smile whenever and wherever you can. Write down how this goes.

_____

_____

_____

_____

_____

_____

_____

_____

_____

_____

_____

_____

_____

_____

Micro Shift #24

Take a good look at your life. Who are you? Where are you at in your life? Why is that?

For better or for worse, your thoughts, actions and, specifically, your decisions have shaped you into who you are. Have you come to love, understand, praise, and if necessary forgive both the person you were in the past as well as the person you are today? If you are finding yourself having difficulty with either, you should remind yourself that it is OK if you have fallen off the path before, as long as you've learned and grown from it.

Once you have come to accept who you are 100%, you will discover a whole new level of inner peace.

Today's Power Phrase:

I will love and accept who I am.

∞

Insight Activity:

What is one area where you've recently fallen off your path? What did you do, say, think, or feel? What part of the situation do you need to forgive yourself for?

_____

_____

_____

_____

_____

_____

_____

_____

_____

_____

_____

_____

_____

_____

_____

Micro Shift #25

How do you react when someone puts pressure on you? Do you remain calm and composed or do you become agitated and violent? How you react in stressful situations is a great indicator of whether or not you are in need of deep reflection and changes in certain areas in your life. Taking a few seconds to think before you respond in those situations could save you from making mistakes which are outside of your normal character. Only when you are healed on the inside will the good come out when the pressure is on.

Today's Power Phrase:

I will work diligently to heal myself from the inside.

Insight Activity:

How did you react the last time you noticed someone put pressure on you? What did you need that you didn't have in that situation? Make a plan now to start to meet that need. Just as you earlier made an appointment with yourself to have some fun, make an appointment with yourself now to reflect and to get that need met.

_____

_____

_____

_____

_____

_____

_____

_____

_____

_____

_____

_____

_____

_____

_____

_____

Micro Shift #26

Life can be very complicated at times. Don't complicate it even more by allowing the thoughts and opinions of others or events outside of your control to affect your day-to-day life. One of the things that you are in absolute control of are your thoughts, so avoid ones that make you feel anything less than the amazing person you are and instead focus on what you can control and thoughts that bring happiness and balance into your life.

Today's Power Phrase:

I will focus my thoughts on what I can control.

Insight Activity:

Have you recently felt brought down in your own energy after taking in the thoughts and opinions of others in your circle? What thoughts and opinions were said, whether of you or situations in general? Which of these made you feel either off center or out of balance? What similar situations might you need to avoid in the future?

_____

_____

_____

_____

_____

_____

_____

_____

_____

_____

_____

_____

_____

_____

_____

_____

Micro Shift #27

If there's one thing I'm sure you and I can relate to, it's that we have faced adversity at one point in time or another. Whatever it is that you've been through in your life, it didn't break you, rather it helped mold you into who you are today. If an experience from your past is still affecting your life, take the time to properly dissect it, and find out how you can start to view it in a constructive way.

The reason that we fall, is so we can learn to pick ourselves back up. Dust your shoulders off, take the information you need from the experience, and continue down the path of improvement.

Today's Power Phrase:

I will learn from my past to build a better future.

∞

Insight Activity:

What is the most recent adverse experience you've been through in the last few weeks or month? Have you taken the time to see what worked in the situation, or steps you might take next time to work toward a better future outcome? If you haven't taken the time to reflect, how about setting a time to do so right now?

_____

_____

_____

_____

_____

_____

_____

_____

_____

_____

_____

_____

_____

_____

Micro Shift #28

At times it can be difficult to decide which path to take in life. When it comes to your journey, it doesn't matter what I say, what your teachers say, what's in the books you read, or what random gossip you hear—unless that information resonates with you and guides you to a place that helps you fulfill your purpose and (of course) makes you happy.

With all of life's distractions, the one person whom you should always be able to rely on to lead you in the right direction is yourself. If you stumble, that's okay. Accept it, learn from it, and continue down the path that is right in front of your eyes.

Today's Power Phrase:

I will be my own best Ally.

∞

Insight Activity:

Do you trust your own inner guidance? Do you make the time to listen to your own inner voice to ensure that the advice and information you take in resonates with your own sense of purpose and your goals? If not, what can you do to create the time and space to check in with yourself? If you already do, how do you rely on your own intuition to guide you to your best decisions?

_____

_____

_____

_____

_____

_____

_____

_____

_____

_____

_____

_____

_____

The best and most beautiful things in the world cannot be
seen or even touched – they must be felt with the heart.

—*Hellen Keller*

Micro Shift #29

Sometimes we underestimate the power our decisions can have. One good decision can send your life to great new heights, while just one bad decision can ruin it forever. You are where you are in your life because of your decisions. Placing the blame on anyone or anything outside of that takes the power to change out of your hands. By taking responsibility for your circumstances and being conscious of your decisions, you will be able to better control the direction your life will go.

Today's Power Phrase:

I will take ownership of my life.

Insight Activity:

What was the best decision you made this past week? What was the result in your life? What part did you play in making that happen? Can you make this a habit?

What about an unwise decision you recently made? How did it turn out? What did you bring to the decision, that might be better to change?

_____

_____

_____

_____

_____

_____

_____

_____

_____

_____

_____

_____

_____

_____

Micro Shift #30

Have you been through a tough experience in your life that you thought you might never recover from? A breakup, a tough new job, or perhaps a loss in the family?

And what did you do? You lived to see another day. You were given the opportunity to learn something from the experience and, if you took advantage of it, you grew as an individual. No matter what life throws your way, do your best to remain optimistic. Remember, what doesn't break you, makes you stronger.

Today's Power Phrase:

I will not allow roadblocks in life to prevent my growth.

Insight Activity:

What was your most recent tough experience? What do you remember telling yourself about the situation? Looking back on it now, did you come through it a little stronger?

Picture a friend going through the same situation. What would you tell him or her to remember about themselves while going through it?

_____

_____

_____

_____

_____

_____

_____

_____

_____

_____

_____

_____

_____

_____

Micro Shift #31

Are you OK with being your authentic self? Freedom is defined as the power or right to act, speak, or think as one
wants without hindrance or restraint. Would you say that
you are free? Or would you say that you are a prisoner to
outside influences? This is your life. If you don't feel that
you have the liberty to live it in a way that brings you happiness, then that is a problem that needs to be addressed. The
people in your life that truly matter will love you for who
you are, so live your life in a way that is going to bring you
the most happiness.

Today's Power Phrase:

I will live my life in the way that brings me the most authentic happiness.

∞

Insight Activity:

Where do you feel just a bit like a prisoner, where you are being "made" to think, or do things that make you feel like less than your free, authentic self? Is there a decision you need to make to change this? A conversation you might need to have?

_____

_____

_____

_____

_____

_____

_____

_____

_____

_____

_____

_____

_____

_____

Micro Shift #32

Do you feel like you're at a standstill in your life? Like you're running on a hamster wheel going nowhere? When you think about your life in all the various areas, like your health, career, and happiness, do you feel like there are some things you might need to do to take them to the next level?

Whether or not to remain in that standstill is a choice you must make, and fortunately so is the decision to change. What are some things you can do to get off the wheel and take things to the next level? Take some time to set up new goals or challenges that will help motivate you to make positive changes in your life.

Today's Power Phrase:

I will always look for ways to move forward in life.

∞

Insight Activity:

Think about three particular situations in your life where you feel stuck. Ask yourself, Are you ready to concentrate on making specific changes in those areas? What can you do (right now) to get started towards making those changes?

_____

_____

_____

_____

_____

_____

_____

_____

_____

_____

_____

_____

_____

_____

Micro Shift #33

Are you currently holding a grudge against someone? A family member, a coworker, or even a crazy ex? Have you ever asked yourself, What is this grudge doing for me? Is it constructive or destructive?

Different scenarios that you encounter call for different actions.

It's common wisdom that positive thoughts lead to positive action, which in turn lead to a positive life.

The next time you find yourself thinking negative thoughts about someone, try your best to flip those thoughts either to something positive about that person, or something that would be a more constructive use of your time and effort.

Today's Power Phrase:

I will hold on to no feelings which bring me down.

∞

Insight Activity:

As you go about your day, who have you noticed you might be holding a grudge against, whether a minor annoyance, or a deeper misgiving? Can you challenge yourself to think of one or two things you appreciate about this person, even though you might still need to work through the irritating situation?

_____

_____

_____

_____

_____

_____

_____

_____

_____

_____

_____

_____

_____

_____

Micro Shift #34

Would you say that what you think, say, and do are all in harmony? It is important we perform periodic self-evaluations every once in a while. These evaluations should include examining the kinds of thoughts you are allowing to dominate your mind, whether what you say to others brings them down or lifts them up, and finally, if your actions are in alignment with your personal integrity.

Doing this will help you maintain your inner peace, so be sure to do it regularly.

Today's Power Phrase:

I will perform regular self-evaluations to ensure I'm living an aligned life.

∞

Insight Activity:

What does self-examination look like for you? Prayer? Meditation? Journaling? Taking a contemplative walk in nature? If you haven't taken time to reflect recently, why not make an appointment with yourself now to do this. Pencil the date and time for this in your calendar.

_____

_____

_____

_____

_____

_____

_____

_____

_____

_____

_____

_____

_____

_____

Micro Shift #35

What are your short-term and long-term goals? Do you have them written out somewhere or have some other means of keeping track of them? Do you hold yourself accountable? Do you reward and reprimand yourself accordingly? These are just a few of the questions you want to ask yourself to ensure that you are on the path that is going to get you to where you want to be. If you know where you want to go in life, it's a lot easier to get there. And once you are there, all that is required is hard work.

Today's Power Phrase:

I will define where I want to be in life and do everything in my power to get there.

Insight Activity:

Take a few minutes to look back at the top three goals you
wrote as part of Micro Shift #21. What small actions did
you set for yourself as a challenge toward those goals? If you
haven't already, set up a checklist or other method to meas-
ure your progress in completing the small daily actions in
the pursuit of your goal.

There is only one success: to be able to spend
life in your own way.

—*Christopher Morley, in*
Where the Blue Begins

Micro Shift #36

Not all of us are experts in math, science, history, or geography; I know I'm not. Does that make us any less special or unique, or mean that we are somehow less deserving or worthy? Of course it doesn't. No one has lived their life in your shoes, so who are they to judge you? Though you might not have discovered it yet, there is something out there you are amazing at—that you were put on this earth to do. Maybe more than one thing. Don't allow anyone or anything to make you feel less than the amazing person that you are.

Today's Power Phrase:

I will embrace that which makes me special.

Insight Activity:

Have you found something you are amazing at? Or at least that you consider yourself pretty good at? Not yet? Has a friend, family member, or anyone ever told you that you do something well? How can you strengthen this sense of confidence or empowerment?

_____

_____

_____

_____

_____

_____

_____

_____

_____

_____

_____

_____

_____

_____

Micro Shift #37

It doesn't matter what your goals for the future are. If your reasons to succeed are not greater than what you are allowing to hold you back, you are fighting a losing battle. What is the most important reason you need to succeed? Not just want to succeed, but truly *have* to succeed. Financial freedom, a better life for your kids, or to be able to say you're the best at something? Whatever that reason is, lock it into your mind, because that is more important than anything which stands in your way. When you are focused and passionate about your success, excuses don't stand a chance.

Today's Power Phrase:

I will always hold on to my reason to succeed.

Insight Activity:

What's your "*why?*" Why do you do what you do? Don't know yet? What can you read, where can you go, who can you dialogue with and trust enough to get their input in helping you find your "why?"

_____

_____

_____

_____

_____

_____

_____

_____

_____

_____

_____

_____

_____

_____

_____

Micro Shift #38

Children, though small, can teach us huge lessons.

Here are a few:

1. Ask, Why? There is so much great information out there. Take in as much as you can.

2. Be honest, even if it's too honest.

3. Don't be afraid to have fun and let loose every once in awhile.

4. Dream big like there is nothing that you cannot do, because the only limits you have are the ones you place on yourself.

Remember that it's OK, and even a little fun to act like a kid sometimes.

Today's Power Phrase:

It's okay to be a kid sometimes.

Insight Activity:

Today, be frank with someone the way a four-year-old can ask a question with no inhibition. Learn from the way a four-year-old asks "Why" dozens of times a day, and asks about how the world works. Ask someone a question about something you've been curious about. Ask a friend. Ask a loved one. Ask Google. Write a bit about what you found.

_____

_____

_____

_____

_____

_____

_____

_____

_____

_____

_____

_____

_____

_____

Micro Shift #39

If you're like me, you have huge goals and dreams but, like the saying goes, "We all have to start somewhere." You may not be a world-renowned speaker, Mr. Olympia, or the CEO of a Fortune 500 company . . . at least not yet and that's OK. What do Tony Robbins, Arnold Schwarzenegger, and Chris Gardner all have in common? They started from the bottom, mastered the basics, and climbed their way to success. It won't happen overnight, but if you work hard, remain patient, and appreciate the journey in addition to success, you will find peace and happiness.

Today's Power Phrase:

I will enjoy every step of my journey to success.

Insight Activity:

Where are you today in your pursuit of the goals and daily steps you've decided to take toward them? With which are you seeing the most progress? Are there any where you might be a bit stuck? What's the next small step you can take to keep going, or to get unstuck? How will you make time to do it today or tomorrow?

_____

_____

_____

_____

_____

_____

_____

_____

_____

_____

_____

_____

_____

_____

Micro Shift #40

The average person speaks thousands of words per day. What kind of impression are your words leaving on others? Do they help them feel better about themselves and empowered or do they put them down? How about when you speak to yourself? Do you reinforce strong positive beliefs and instill faith, or do you cause more doubt and fear to arise? Words have inspired great changes in this world, both positive and negative. Be sure to use yours to build yourself and others up and make this world a better place.

Today's Power Phrase:

I will use my words to create positive change.

Insight Activity:

Think back over your conversations with others today. Did they lift others up? If your friends were to pass along to others the same things you say to them, would they feel uplifted, or brought down a bit? What about what you said to yourself?

_____

_____

_____

_____

_____

_____

_____

_____

_____

_____

_____

_____

_____

Micro Shift #41

What were you put on this earth to do? For some this is the million-dollar question. In life sometimes we have to do what we have to do to survive and support ourselves and our families. But sometimes we become so consumed with that idea that we forget that there is something more . . . our passion. Doing something that brings us joy and inner peace, and gives us a sense of fulfillment. There's absolutely nothing wrong with doing what you have to do, but don't let that idea overshadow the pursuit of your dreams and the fulfillment of your purpose.

Today's Power Phrase:

I will do what I have to do but not at the expense of my happiness and dreams.

∞

Insight Activity:

How can you make time to do both what you "have" to do and what you "want" to do?

Now, write down (again) what you were put on this Earth to do? How will you take time today or tomorrow to take the next action or two to bring about that purpose?

_____

_____

_____

_____

_____

_____

_____

_____

_____

_____

_____

_____

_____

_____

_____

Micro Shift #42

Do you make the most of your free time? Outside of the eight hours you possibly get for sleep, and the eight hours you spend at work, how do you allocate the remaining eight hours of your day?

One of the most empowering things you can do to make the most of your day is to write out a to-do list—a list of all the things you should be doing on a regular basis, to get where you want to go in life. Once you have that it all comes down to the self-discipline and integrity to accomplish the things you wrote down.

Today's Power Phrase:

I will ensure that my free time is utilized for my progression.

∞

Insight Activity:

Have you written a to-do list for today, or tomorrow? Is it balanced between the vital areas of your life (i.e. work, family, recreation, spiritual reconnection?). Are you getting done what you want to get done?

If so, fantastic! If not, what adjustments might you need to make? And . . . are you remembering to include next steps towards your larger goals and dreams?

_____

_____

_____

_____

_____

_____

_____

_____

_____

_____

_____

_____

_____

The future belongs to those who believe
in the beauty of their dreams.

—*Eleanor Roosevelt*

Micro Shift #43

Honesty is a great practice, and the most important person you must be honest with is yourself. Being honest with yourself will help you in many ways along the path to self-improvement. It will help you properly gauge where you are and what you need to improve. It will prevent you from playing it too safe as well as from setting yourself up for failure. It will also help you to maintain your integrity and discipline by doing what you know in your heart to be right. Do your best to make honesty a priority in your life. You won't regret it.

Today's Power Phrase:

I will make honesty a core principle in my life.

∞

Insight Activity:

Today, take a few minutes to get quiet. In that quiet space, check in with yourself: Am I being open and honest with those closest to me? Is there a conversation I need to have I might be putting off?

Am I being honest with myself? Am I paying attention to, and following, my intuition? Are there any healthy "shoulds" I've been trying not to look at, but that continue to arise in my mind?

_____

_____

_____

_____

_____

_____

_____

_____

_____

_____

_____

_____

Micro Shift #44

What are the limits of your potential? This is a question that you, and only you can determine the answer to. No one else can ever fully know what you are capable of. Human beings have continuously surpassed all limitations, and continue to break barriers most "knew" were impossible. Be sure that you are not creating any of these psychological barriers in your life—the kind of barriers that limit the far-reaching powers of our imagination. Be the one that laughs at obstacles and yells Bring them on!

Today's Power Phrase:

I will view obstacles as stepping stones to Greatness.

Insight Activity:

When was the last time you shared a goal or aspiration with someone, and they tried to talk you out of it, no matter how subtle, or how "well-meaning" they were in their intent? What did they say?

Too, did you try talking yourself out of the goal? What did you say to yourself? Take time right now to brainstorm three action steps to prove them (and yourself) wrong.

_____

_____

_____

_____

_____

_____

_____

_____

_____

_____

_____

_____

_____

Micro Shift #45

There is a reason that we don't live forever. If we did, certain things such as making the most of each day, valuing the time we share with loved ones, and appreciating every one of life's tiny blessings would lose their value. Mortality is just one of those blessings in life that are often overlooked. Every single part of life, even the fact that it ends is, from a certain perspective, beautiful. With that in mind do your best to make the most of each day and live your life to the fullest.

Today's Power Phrase:

I will view every moment as a blessing.

Insight Activity:

As you are going through your day, take a moment to imagine that you have one week to live. What would you miss?

From this new vantage point, what is something that seemed insignificant when compared with deadlines, social media, and similar "obligations," but that takes on more importance in the context of fewer days? What do you notice that you might be taking for granted?

_____

_____

_____

_____

_____

_____

_____

_____

_____

_____

_____

_____

Micro Shift #46

It is said that you are the average of the five people that you spend the most time with. How have your associations affected your life? Do the people closest to you fill you with love and confidence, and help you to feel at peace, or do you find yourself feeling insecure and being deterred from progress? Ensure that the people you allow into your inner circle complement the lifestyle you want for yourself and encourage you to strive for greatness. Your associations can either be a gift or a crutch; be sure to choose yours wisely.

Today's Power Phrase:

I will seek associations that encourage my growth.

Insight Activity:

Make the list of the five people closest to you, those you spend the most time with throughout the week. Pay attention to how you feel after the next time you talk with one of them. Do you feel there is a need to make some changes to your circle of associations?

_____

_____

_____

_____

_____

_____

_____

_____

_____

_____

_____

_____

_____

Micro Shift #47

Faith is defined as a belief in something for which there is no proof. It is an essential concept, especially if you are seeking to achieve Greatness. Whatever your idea of Greatness is, it is just that . . . an idea. Faith is the magic that will turn that idea into a reality.

The way that you will strengthen your faith is with consistent actions that are in alignment with your endgame. It may not happen overnight, but with faith and optimism, you will enjoy every step of the journey.

Today's Power Phrase:

I have faith that I will achieve Greatness.

Insight Activity:

Do you have faith in the self-confidence and self-assurance that you need in order to go after your greatest goals? If not, what might help you bolster these two essential attributes?

Today, what is the smallest first step that will help you "Act as if" and get back on the path to what you want to achieve, even if you feel you have to "fake it" for the time being?

_____

_____

_____

_____

_____

_____

_____

_____

_____

_____

_____

_____

_____

Micro Shift #48

There are times in our lives when we have so much going on that we are not fully able to appreciate everything that is happening in the present moment. It is during these times that you should practice the art of mindfulness.

Mindfulness is a technique in which you focus your attention only on the present—experiencing thoughts, feelings, and sensations without judgment. Being able to fully immerse yourself in the actions of the present moment will improve the quality of your relationships, enhance your mental and physical well-being, and greatly assist you in realizing the magnificence that each day brings.

Today's Power Phrase:

I will fully immerse myself in the present.

∞

Insight Activity:

Today, take a few minutes to practice being more present and mindful of where you are. Try closing your eyes and paying attention to the sensation of each breath as it passes in and out of your nostrils. Perhaps even try counting each breath, from one to ten.

Another way to be present is to focus on a specific part of the body. As you eat your next meal, take a moment to take in the unique smells, the texture and taste of each bite as it hits your tongue, and the satisfying feeling after each bite.

What are some other simple five-minute ways you can bring more mindfulness to your day?

_____

_____

_____

_____

_____

_____

_____

_____

_____

Micro Shift #49

Would you say that you are well disciplined? As human beings, we have certain default settings, and one of those settings is the seeking of pleasure and the avoidance of pain.
This is known as the pain-pleasure principle . . . go figure.
Having discipline will allow you to bend that principle to
your will.

The key to doing this is ensuring that you associate
more pleasure with the action that is going to help move you
to where you want to go. This may seem like something that
is easier said than done, but, just like building a muscle it will
become easier with time. You also want to ensure that you
keep your purpose at the core of your mind. Your probabil-
ity of success will come down to how passionate you are to
achieve it.

Today's Power Phrase:

Mastering my discipline will help me become my best self.

∞

Insight Activity:

Revisit your lists of things that need to be done, both those next actions aimed to bring you toward completion of your highest goals, and some that are more everyday necessities. Of these, which are you least looking forward to? How can you increase your discipline in taking the next step to get it done? Do you need to perhaps set a reward for getting it done? Do you need to simply sit in front of it and "stare" at it for a few minutes until you are prompted to take action?

_____

_____

_____

_____

_____

_____

_____

_____

_____

_____

_____

_____

_____

Take Action! An inch of movement will bring you closer to your goals than a mile of intention.

—*Steve Maraboli, in*
Unapologetically You

Micro Shift #50

I could deliver to you the greatest and most motivating speech you've ever heard in your life, or write the most inspiring book but it would mean absolutely nothing if you didn't believe in yourself. If you monitor your thoughts for the day, how often are you thinking about your ability to succeed as opposed to failing? The true percentage should give you a good gauge of where you are, and if necessary motivate you to make changes. If you don't believe in your own ability to achieve your goals, then you are the hamster on the wheel, running full speed to nowhere. But if you have faith in yourself, there is nothing that can stop you from ascending to greatness. You are an infinite being that is capable of achieving anything. Don't think you are—know you are and claim the greatness you so incredibly deserve.

Today's Power Phrase:

I am an infinite being, worthy of love and capable of achieving anything.

∞

Insight Activity:

Try finding out for yourself whether your own thoughts are positive and filled with faith, or perhaps filled with fear and anxiety. Take a journal or legal pad, and pen. Set the timer on your phone for five minutes. Close your eyes for a moment, and pay attention to the stream of thoughts in your mind.

When you can notice what these thoughts are, word for word, then start the timer, and start writing down these thoughts exactly as they are in your head word for word—verbatim. At the end of the five minutes . . . go over what you wrote. Are they largely positive, somewhat negative, perhaps somewhere in-between?

Is this where you want to be?

_____

_____

_____

_____

_____

_____

_____

_____

_____

Message from the Author

I would like to congratulate you on your completion of this journey. It is my great hope that the concepts that have been shared here have brought happiness, inner peace, and love into your life. The reinforcement of positive information is similar to a workout: The more that you do, the easier it gets and the stronger you become. I would like for you to view this as not the end of a journey, but simply the beginning of a lifelong mission of becoming your greatest self and maintaining that perspective and lifestyle. Understand that you are a being of unlimited potential. There are no limits that we don't create ourselves. I hope you are as excited as I am about the great things which you shall accomplish. That statement might leave you feeling a bit curious but, as I stated before, this world will not live up to its true potential unless we all strive to become our greatest selves and then turn our attention to creating a greater world and building one another up to achieve the same.

I would love to know more about your journey with *The Greatness Effect*. Please feel free to reach out to me at trwspeaks.com to give me your feedback and to find out additional ways to continue your personal development. Additionally, if you found this book to be of value, I would be very grateful if you would consider writing a book review on Amazon.com. I am hopeful that I will have the pleasure of assisting you in the future with your pursuit of becoming your best self. I will leave you with these words: "You are a human being, who is worthy of love, happiness, and success." Know, Understand, and Embrace that philosophy and you will know Greatness.

About Timothy Wallace

Mr. Wallace is a Certified Life Coach, Motivational Speaker, and an Active Duty member of the United States Navy. He began his journey of self-improvement in January of 2010 when he enlisted into the military as an Air Traffic Controller, considered to be one of the most stressful jobs in the world. His time in the service taught him the importance of having clearly defined objectives, establishing unwavering barriers and having discipline, and that without self-love and respect, it is extremely difficult to excel.

Living a life filled with adversity also instilled within him a desire to help those less fortunate, as well as individuals in need of guidance in achieving positive changes in their lives. In doing so he found his life's purpose and has now devoted his life to helping people achieve self-mastery and personal freedom. For more information on Mr. Wallace and his services visit trwspeaks.com.

You can also follow TRWSpeaks on Facebook, Twitter, and Instagram:

https://www.facebook.com/trwspeaks
https://twitter.com/trwspeaks
Instagram: @trwspeaks